When to Pray

Everyone Needs a Little Jesus

A 5-Day Prayer Guide

Sally Larkin Green

Lordship Community Church

Copyright Page

When to Pray: Everyone Needs a Little Jesus
© 2025 by Sally Larkin Green

Scripture Quotations: Scripture quotations taken from the **Holy Bible, New International Version®, NIV®**. Copyright © 1973, 1978, 1984, 2011 by Biblica, Inc. Used by permission. All rights reserved worldwide.

For more information about NIV, visit: www.Biblica.com

Unless otherwise noted, emphasis in Scripture quotations is the author's own.

ISBN: 979-8-9985211-0-2

Printed in the United States of America

For information, speaking requests, or additional resources, visit:
⊕ FindSally.com   Email: sally@actiontakerspublishing.com

Table of Contents

A Note from the Author

My story with Lordship Community Church began in the early 1980's, just after my husband and I got engaged. It was a season of growth at the church, with pews filled and Sunday School classrooms overflowing. Even though I had very little Bible knowledge, I felt God calling me to step up when the pastor asked for Sunday School teachers. That small "yes" turned into more than 30 years of teaching, writing, guiding, and pouring into the next generation.

I've seen the church at its strongest, and I've felt the ache of decline. I've taught classes of 50 children, and I've taught three children of very different ages. Through it all, the joy of teaching never left me. Watching students light up when they learned about Jesus, lit something inside of me. But God began stirring something new in me. A call to step into leadership, to preach, and to help shepherd the church I love.

Along the way, prayer has been one of the hardest and holiest lessons of my life. I've stumbled. I've doubted. I've wondered if my words mattered. Yet, I discovered this truth: God isn't looking for polished words, He's looking for willing hearts.

That's why I wrote this book. Not because I have all the answers, but because I want to walk with you as we learn together. Prayer isn't about perfection, it's about presence. My hope is that you'll discover the same thing I have: you don't have to be perfect at prayer. You just have to begin.

Sally Larkin Green

Introduction – When to Pray

Prayer is talking to God like you would to a trusted friend: simple, candid, and real. Yet for many of us, it doesn't always feel natural.

We wonder: Am I doing this right? What if I say the wrong thing? Should I kneel? Should I fold my hands? Should my eyes be closed? Do I need to sound official or holy?

Then we read, "Pray without ceasing" (1 Thessalonians 5:17), and we wonder how is that even possible?!

But maybe prayer isn't about praying longer or louder. Maybe it's simply about showing up and talking to God as we are, wherever we are, with whatever is on our hearts.

Over the next five days, this book will guide you through different biblical examples of prayer: Hannah's honesty, Jonah's desperation, Jesus' blueprint, and the invitation to pray in both ordinary and peaceful moments.

My prayer is that by the end, you will see prayer not as a ritual to master, but as a simple, life-changing way to draw closer to Jesus.

Because everyone needs a little Jesus.

Reader Bonus: A Gift for You

Want to keep growing in your prayer life?
Here's a simple resource just for you:

5 Ways to Pray: A Simple Guide

This easy-to-follow guide will show you five practical ways you
can bring prayer into your everyday life, whether you're at
home, at work, or on the go.

👉 To claim your free copy,

Go to <u>SallyLarkinGreen.com</u> and register today.

Day 1 – Pray Like Hannah: Pouring Out Your Soul When You're Broken

Read Scripture: *1 Samuel 1:9–18*

Psalm Connection: *Psalm 34:17–18 – The righteous cry out, and the Lord hears them; he delivers them from all their troubles. The Lord is close to the brokenhearted and saves those who are crushed in spirit.*

Hannah's husband loved her, but she had no children. In her culture, that was seen as a disgrace, and to make it worse, her husband's other wife never let her forget it.

Year after year, Hannah went to the temple and cried. She was exhausted, discouraged, and running out of hope. One day, in the middle of her grief, she broke down and prayed.

It wasn't loud or fancy, just a whisper as she cried to the Lord. She was so quiet the priest thought she was drunk. But Hannah said, *"I was pouring out my soul to the Lord."* (1 Samuel 1:15)

She walked away still childless, **yet different.** Scripture says her face was no longer downcast. *That's the power of prayer. It doesn't always change our circumstances right away, but it changes us.*

In time, God answered her prayer and Hannah gave birth to Samuel. Samuel would become one of Israel's greatest leaders. It all started with one woman's quiet, heartbroken, tear-filled prayer.

Reflection/Journal Questions

1. What disappointment or pain do you need to pour out to God today?

2. How might honesty, not perfection, change your prayers this week?

Prayer

Lord,
You are close to the brokenhearted, and today I come to you with my hurts. Like Hannah, I bring the disappointments that are weighing me down, the longings that remain unmet, and the tears that sometimes feel endless. I don't want to hide from you or pretend to be strong. I want to pour out my soul before you. Hear my cry and meet me with your peace. Even before the answers come, remind me that you are near, and that is enough.

Amen.

Action Step

Write out one raw, unfiltered prayer. Don't edit it, just pour it out.

Day 2 – Pray Like Jonah: Crying Out for Help When You're Desperate

Read Scripture: Jonah 2:1–10

Psalm Connection: *Psalm 18:4–6 The cords of death entangled me; the torrents of destruction overwhelmed me. The cords of the grave coiled around me; the snares of death confronted me. In my distress I called to the LORD; I cried to my God for help. From his temple he heard my voice; my cry came before him, into his ears.*

God called Jonah to go to Nineveh, but Jonah fled the Lord's command and ran the other way. It wasn't until he ended up in the belly of a fish, with seaweed wrapped around his head, that Jonah finally prayed.

Jonah's prayer wasn't pretty, it was desperate. But God still heard him and delivered him back to dry land.

Jonah's prayer reminds us that even in the moments when we're trying to run away, even in places where we feel swallowed up by doubt or fear, God is still listening. Our prayers don't need polish, they need to be real and from the heart. Just a conversation with God.

You can pray like Jonah. You can cry out in fear and desperation. You can admit your failures, and God will meet you there, lifting you up from the belly of the whale and reminding you that when God has called you, his opportunities come with his strength.

Reflection / Journal Questions

1. When have you felt "swallowed up" by fear, doubt, or failure?

2. What keeps you from praying openly in those moments of desperation?

Prayer

Lord,

I confess that sometimes I run from the things you ask of me. I let fear, doubt, and feelings of inadequacy keep me from trusting you fully. But even when I run, you are still listening. Even when I feel trapped by circumstances, you are near. Like Jonah, I cry out to you today: hear my prayer, Lord, and lift me out of the pit. Remind me that your strength is enough for every calling and every challenge. I choose to trust you, even when I don't feel qualified.

Amen.

Action Step

Today, take one fear or area of doubt in your life and pray about it openly. Don't polish the words, just tell God exactly how you feel.

Day 3 – Pray Like Jesus: A Blueprint for Prayer When You're Unsure

Read Scripture: *Matthew 6:5–13*
Psalm Connection: *Psalm 145:18–19 The Lord is near to all who call on him, to all who call on him in truth. He fulfills the desires of those who fear him; he hears their cry and saves them.*

In Matthew 6, right in the middle of the Sermon on the Mount, Jesus paused to talk about prayer. He said, *"When you pray, don't be like the hypocrites who love to stand on the street corners to be seen by others."* He warned against long, showy prayers filled with empty words.

Then he gave us something simple, powerful, and enduring: the Lord's Prayer.

So how can you pray? You can pray exactly as Jesus taught, especially when you are unsure what to say. Or you can let his words serve as a pattern to guide your own conversations with God, one step at a time. You do not have to start from scratch. Jesus already gave us the blueprint.

The Lord's Prayer

Matthew 6:9–13 (NIV)

Our Father in heaven,
hallowed be your name,
your kingdom come,
your will be done,
on earth as it is in heaven.
Give us today our daily bread.
And forgive us our debts,
as we also have forgiven our debtors.
And lead us not into temptation,
but deliver us from the evil one.

Amen.

Here's a breakdown of how we can pray using the pattern Jesus gave us:

- **Start with praise** – *"Our Father in heaven, hallowed be your name."*
- **Surrender your plans** – *"Your kingdom come, your will be done, on earth as it is in heaven."*
- **Ask for what you need** – *"Give us this day our daily bread."*
- **Seek forgiveness** – *"Forgive us our debts, as we forgive our debtors."*
- **Ask for strength** – *"Deliver us from evil."*

Reflection / Journal Questions

1. Which part of the Lord's Prayer feels most personal to your life right now?

2. How could you use this prayer as a daily rhythm this week?

Prayer

Our Father in heaven, hallowed be Your name. Today I begin with praise, remembering who you are and how good you have been to me. I surrender my will to yours

Your kingdom come, your will be done in my life. Provide what I need today, Lord, and give me a heart of gratitude for every blessing.

Forgive me where I have fallen short, and teach me to forgive others with the same grace you have shown me. Strengthen me against temptation, and deliver me from evil. I trust you as my Father and King.

Amen.

Action Step

Pray the Lord's Prayer once a day this week. Then rewrite it in your own words, making each phrase personal to your life.

Jeremiah 29:12

"Then you will call on me and come and pray to me, and I will listen to you."

Day 4 – Everyday Prayer: Talking With God in Ordinary Moments

Read Scripture: *1 Thessalonians 5:16–18*
Psalm Connection: *Psalm 139:1–3 You have searched for me, Lord, and you know me. You know when I sit and when I rise; you perceive my thoughts from afar. You discern my going out and my lying down; you are familiar with all my ways.*

Prayer is not reserved for Sunday mornings or moments of crisis. It belongs in every corner of our lives. Prayer can rise from the kitchen sink washing dishes, from the driver's seat on the morning commute, from a school desk before a test, or from the stillness of the night when sleep will not come. God hears whispered prayers, messy prayers that spill out in tears, and unfinished prayers that fade into silence. He does not require us to sound holy or polished. He simply wants our hearts.

At Lordship Community Church, we have seen prayer happen everywhere: in the pews on Sunday, around kitchen tables during family meals, in circles at church meetings, and in hospital waiting rooms filled with both fear and hope. Some prayers have been shouted with joy, others have been spoken softly, and still others lifted only in silence. Every single one was real, and every single one was heard.

The truth is, God already knows us completely. He knows when we rise and when we lie down. He knows our thoughts, our routines, our worries, and our joys. He is not distant, waiting for perfect words. He is with us and ready to meet us exactly where we are.

Reflection / Journal Questions

1. Where in your daily routine could you invite God into prayer?

2. What would it look like if you treated prayer as an ongoing conversation rather than a once-in-a-while practice?

Prayer

Lord,

Thank you for being with me in the ordinary places of my life. You know when I wake and when I rest, when I feel rushed and when I feel still. Teach me to bring you into my daily life, not just the big moments but the small ones too. Let me remember that I can talk to you while doing ordinary things, the drive to work, or sitting quietly at the end of the day. Fill my ordinary moments with your extraordinary presence, and let prayer become the steady heartbeat of my life.

Amen.

Action Step

Choose one ordinary task this week; making your morning coffee, driving to work, walking the dog ... and turn it into a time of prayer.

Day 5 – Prayer is a Relationship: Drawing Near When You Need Peace

Read Scripture: *Philippians 4:6–7*
Psalm Connection: *Psalm 62:8 Trust in him at all times, you people; pour out your hearts to him, for God is our refuge.*

Hannah shows us we can pray through heartbreak. Jonah shows us we can pray in desperation. Jesus shows us we can pray with purpose and make it a daily habit. Together, these stories remind us that prayer is not about performance. It is about a relationship with God.

Prayer is not a formula to master. It is not a ritual to check off a list. It is the living, ongoing connection between you and God. He is not grading your words. He is listening to your heart.

When you begin to see prayer this way, it becomes less about "doing it right" and more about being with God. He wants honesty, not perfection. He wants presence, not polish. The more you bring your whole self to him, the more you discover his peace, his guidance, and his love.

And the more you pray, the more natural it becomes. Prayer begins to weave itself into the rhythm of your life: in the car, in the kitchen, in the quiet moments before sleep. It becomes less about finding the perfect words and more about noticing God's presence in every moment. Prayer isn't something we master once…it's a lifelong conversation with the God who loves us most.

Reflection / Journal Questions

1. What holds you back from praying freely and openly with God?

2. How would your prayer life change if you treated it less like a ritual and more like a relationship?

Prayer

Lord,

Thank you for reminding me that you are not looking for perfect words but for an open heart. Forgive me for the times I have treated prayer like a task instead of a relationship. Teach me to come to you sincerely, with trust and love. When I feel anxious, help me bring everything to you and rest in your peace. Let prayer be the rhythm of my life, a daily conversation that draws me closer to you.

Amen.

Action Step

Try praying in a new way, write a prayer in your journal, sing a prayer, whisper a prayer while you walk, or simply sit in silence. Notice how God meets you in the moment.

The Power of Prayer

Prayer begins with willingness. Hannah showed us how to pour out our soul when we are broken. Jonah reminded us that even in desperation, God still hears. Jesus gave us a blueprint for prayer when we feel unsure of what to pray. **We discovered how to invite God into the ordinary moments of our daily lives, and we learned that prayer is not a ritual but a relationship that brings peace.**

This 5-day journey isn't the end, it's the beginning. Prayer is not something we "finish" or graduate from. It is the ongoing conversation of a lifetime. **As you practice, prayer weaves into your days until talking with God feels as natural as breathing.**

So keep going. Keep pouring out your heart. Keep crying out when you are desperate. Keep leaning on the words Jesus gave us. Keep noticing God's presence in the ordinary. **Keep drawing near to him for peace.**

Prayer is not about getting the words right.

It is about drawing closer to Jesus. And when you do, you will find he is already closer to you than you ever imagined

And that's why ...

Everyone Needs a Little Jesus

Appendix A: Scripture Readings
Day 1 – Pray Like Hannah: Pouring Out Your Soul When You're Broken

1 Samuel 1:9–18 (NIV)

Once when they had finished eating and drinking in Shiloh, Hannah stood up. Now Eli the priest was sitting on his chair by the doorpost of the Lord's house. In her deep anguish Hannah prayed to the Lord, weeping bitterly. And she made a vow, saying, "Lord Almighty, if you will only look on your servant's misery and remember me, and not forget your servant but give her a son, then I will give him to the Lord for all the days of his life, and no razor will ever be used on his head."

As she kept on praying to the Lord, Eli observed her mouth. Hannah was praying in her heart, and her lips were moving but her voice was not heard. Eli thought she was drunk and said to her, "How long are you going to stay drunk? Put away your wine."

"Not so, my lord," Hannah replied, "I am a woman who is deeply troubled. I have not been drinking wine or beer; I was pouring out my soul to the Lord. Do not take your servant for a wicked woman; I have been praying here out of my great anguish and grief."

Eli answered, "Go in peace, and may the God of Israel grant you what you have asked of him."

She said, "May your servant find favor in your eyes." Then she went her way and ate something, and her face was no longer downcast.

Day 2 – Pray Like Jonah: Crying Out for Help When You're Desperate

Jonah 2:1–10 (NIV)

From inside the fish Jonah prayed to the Lord his God. He said:

"In my distress I called to the Lord, and he answered me.
From deep in the realm of the dead I called for help,
and you listened to my cry.
You hurled me into the depths,
into the very heart of the seas,
and the currents swirled about me;
all your waves and breakers swept over me.
I said, 'I have been banished from your sight;
yet I will look again toward your holy temple.'
The engulfing waters threatened me,
the deep surrounded me;
seaweed was wrapped around my head.
To the roots of the mountains I sank down;
the earth beneath barred me forever.
But you, Lord my God,
brought my life up from the pit.

"When my life was ebbing away,
I remembered you, Lord,
and my prayer rose to you,
to your holy temple.

"Those who cling to worthless idols
turn away from God's love for them.
But I, with shouts of grateful praise,
will sacrifice to you.
What I have vowed I will make good.
I will say, 'Salvation comes from the Lord.'"

And the Lord commanded the fish, and it vomited Jonah onto dry land.

Matthew 7:7

"Ask and it will be given to you; seek and you will find; knock and the door will be opened to you."

Day 3 – Pray Like Jesus: A Blueprint for Prayer When You're Unsure

Matthew 6:5–13 (NIV)

"And when you pray, do not be like the hypocrites, for they love to pray standing in the synagogues and on the street corners to be seen by others. Truly I tell you, they have received their reward in full. But when you pray, go into your room, close the door and pray to your Father, who is unseen. Then your Father, who sees what is done in secret, will reward you.

And when you pray, do not keep on babbling like pagans, for they think they will be heard because of their many words. Do not be like them, for your Father knows what you need before you ask him.

This, then, is how you should pray:

Our Father in heaven,
hallowed be your name,
your kingdom come,
your will be done,
on earth as it is in heaven.
Give us today our daily bread.
And forgive us our debts,
as we also have forgiven our debtors.
And lead us not into temptation,
but deliver us from the evil one.

Day 4 – Everyday Prayer: Talking With God in Ordinary Moments

1 Thessalonians 5:16–18 (NIV)
Rejoice always, pray continually, give thanks in all circumstances; for this is God's will for you in Christ Jesus.

Day 5 – Prayer Is a Relationship: Drawing Near When You Need Peace

Philippians 4:6–7 (NIV)
Do not be anxious about anything, but in every situation, by prayer and petition, with thanksgiving, present your requests to God. And the peace of God, which transcends all understanding, will guard your hearts and your minds in Christ Jesus.

Romans 12:12

*"Be joyful in hope, patient in affliction,
faithful in prayer."*

Appendix B : Sermon: *How Do I Pray?*

Sermon Delivered at Lordship Community Church
August 31, 2025

Prayer is talking to God like you would to a trusted friend, honest, simple, and real.

It doesn't always feel that natural. Sometimes it can feel awkward, intimidating, or even confusing

Many of us feel unsure we're praying right.

We wonder: *Am I supposed to say certain words? What if I mess it up? Do I have to kneel? Pray with my hands clasped? Close my eyes? Does it have to sound official or holy?*

And then we read verses like *"Pray without ceasing"* (1 Thessalonians 5:17), and it feels overwhelming.

I'm supposed to pray ... All the time? Without stopping? How is that even possible?

But maybe it's not about praying longer or louder.

Maybe it's just about **talking to God**, as we are, wherever we are, with whatever's on our heart.

I remember the first time I was invited to a prayer group. It was back in 2006. I was in my 40s and had been teaching Sunday School for years, but I had never really prayed out loud.

Not once. Unless you count the prayers that were printed at the bottom of the Sunday school lessons I taught.

This group I was invited to... they were praying for a teen Bible study to come to Connecticut.

And I thought, *"Sure, I'll sit in and listen."* What I didn't know was that I'd be expected to pray.
Out loud.
In front of other adults.
Off the top of my head.
No script. No reading. No Nothing!
Just me and my words.

Honestly? I was terrified.

The first few weeks, I stayed quiet. I bowed my head, nodded along, and hoped no one would call on me.
But the Holy Spirit ... knows how to stir things up.

By the 3rd or 4th week, something shifted. I opened my mouth and prayed. It was short. It was choppy.
But it was *mine.* And it was *real.*

Before long, I wasn't just praying, I was dreaming up ways for our group to take action.

And you know what? I'm still there.
Praying out loud, off the top of my head, still isn't something I'm great at.
But writing prayers? That's something I can do.

So if you're sitting here today thinking, *"I don't know how to pray"* you are not alone.

It doesn't have to be polished.
You just have to begin and be willing.

And it seems that's been the theme all summer ... **beginning and being willing to step up**, being willing to open your bible, being willing to share Jesus with others, and being willing to sing. Being willing to show up on Sunday.

And today ... **being willing to pray.**

God isn't looking for perfect people.
He's just looking for people who are willing.

Today, I'm going to share **some different prayers in the Bible**.

I want to begin with how to pray when we're stressed and have hit rock bottom. Let's look at a woman named **Hannah**.

Hannah was heartbroken. She was married to a man named Elkanah, who loved her deeply, but she had no children. In that time and culture, being childless was seen as a disgrace. To make things worse, her husband's other wife had many children and constantly bullied and ridiculed Hannah.

Year after year, they would travel to the temple to worship, and year after year, Hannah cried. Her heart ached. Her hope was fading. The Bible tells us she was "deeply troubled" and "wept bitterly." She wasn't just sad, she was *exhausted by disappointment.*

Then one day, in the middle of her grief, Hannah did something powerful.

She broke down in the temple, unable to hold back her tears, she began to pray.

It wasn't loud or polished. In fact, it was so quiet the priest, Eli, saw her lips moving - heard no sound and assumed she was drunk. That's how crazy she looked.

When Eli approached her, Hannah replied:

> "I was pouring out my soul to the Lord." (1 Samuel 1:15)

She wasn't putting on a show. She was laying her pain and anguish before God. She wasn't trying to hold it together, she was letting it all out.

And God heard her.

She left that temple still childless, but she was changed. The Scripture in verse 18 says, *"She went her way and ate something, and her face was no longer downcast."*

That's the power of prayer. *It doesn't always change our circumstances right away, but it can change us and bring us peace before the answer comes.*

In time, God did answer. And Hannah gave birth to a son named **Samuel**.

Samuel would grow up to be a prophet, a priest, and a judge. He would anoint **King Saul** and **King David**. He would become a spiritual leader for the nation of Israel.

And it all started with one woman's quiet, tear-filled prayer.

So how can you pray?

You can pray like Hannah.

You can come to God hurting, misunderstood, and unsure and still be heard.

And sometimes the most powerful prayer starts with this simple surrender:

"God, here's what I'm feeling, help me!"

And that's more than enough.

If Hannah shows us how to pray from the heart, Jonah shows us how to pray in desperation.

Jonah was a prophet, called by God to go to Nineveh, but he didn't feel qualified. He didn't want the job. So he ran. He literally boarded a ship going in the opposite direction. And you know the story, during a storm he was tossed overboard and Jonah ends up in the belly of a great fish.

And it's there, in the dark, with seaweed wrapped around his head, fearing for this life, that Jonah finally prays. The Bible records his words in Jonah chapter 2:

> *"In my distress I called to the Lord, and he answered me.*
> *From deep in the realm of the dead I called for help,*
> *and you listened to my cry…*
> *But you, Lord my God,*
> *brought my life up from the pit.*
> *When my life was ebbing away, I remembered you, Lord,*
> *and my prayer rose to you, to your holy temple."*
> (Jonah 2:2, 6–7)

That prayer wasn't pretty. It wasn't polished. It was desperate. And when Jonah's prayer was finished, God delivered him safely back onto dry land.

I'll be honest with you, I feel a lot like Jonah. I don't feel qualified to do the things God is calling me to do. There are days I think, *"Surely there's someone else who could do this better."*

Running away often seems like a much easier option.

But here's what Jonah reminds me: **even in the moments when we're trying to run away, even in places where we feel swallowed up by doubt or fear, God is still listening.** Our prayers don't have to be perfect, they just have to be real and from the heart. Just a conversation with God.

You can pray like Jonah. You can cry out in fear and desperation. You can admit your failures, and God will meet you there … lifting you up from the belly of the whale and reminding you that **his opportunities come with his strength.**

Jonah's story reminds us that even when we're running, God still listens. But Jesus teaches us something more: that prayer isn't just for emergencies, it's meant to be added to our daily routine.

In Matthew 6, right in the middle of the Sermon on the Mount, Jesus pauses to talk about prayer. He tells his followers, *"When you pray, don't be like the hypocrites who love to stand on the street corners to be seen by others."* He warns against long, showy prayers filled with empty words. And then, he gives us something so simple, and so powerful—it has echoed through history.

> *"This, then, is how you should pray…"* (Matthew 6:9)
> and he gives us the Lord's Prayer.

So how can you pray?
You can pray like Jesus taught us.
You can use the words exactly - when you're not sure what else to say.
Or you can let them guide your own conversation with God, one section at a time.

Start with praise. (hallowed be thy name)
Surrender your plans (Thy will be done).
Ask for what you need. (Give us this day our daily bread)
Seek forgiveness. (Forgive us our debts)
Ask for strength. (Deliver us from evil)

You don't have to start from scratch.
Jesus already gave you the blueprint!

Hannah shows us that we can pray through pain and heartbreak. That our tears count. That silent prayers are still heard.

Jonah shows us that we can pray when you feel trapped, desperate, unqualified, or we feel like running away. That even in the darkest places, God still hears us.

And Jesus shows us that you can pray with purpose, knowing that God is near. Jesus gave us the exact words to say when we feel unsure about how to pray.

So the answer to ... how do we pray?
Is ... however you need to.

With emotion. With structure. With songs.
With a journal, or a whisper, or a desperate "Help me!"

You can pray in the car. In the kitchen. In the middle of the night. With your Bible open. Or with nothing but your breath and the faith of a mustard seed.

Because prayer isn't a formula. It's a relationship.

It's not about doing it right, it's about doing it.

And the God you're talking to?
He's not grading your words.
He's listening to your heart.

And maybe when you pray this week, whether it's a whisper, a cry, or the words Jesus taught us, you'll notice what I noticed last week. That Prayer is a reminder that God is here, he hears you, and he loves you.

Appendix C: Group Discussion Questions

Day 1 – Hannah: Pouring Out Your Soul
When You're Broken

1. Why do you think Hannah's prayer, though quiet and tear-filled, was so powerful?

2. Have you ever felt misunderstood in your prayers, like Hannah was by Eli? How did you handle it?

3. What does it mean to "pour out your soul" before God in your own life?

4. How can prayer bring peace even before circumstances change?

5. Share a time when you felt God heard you even though the answer hadn't come yet.

Day 2 – Jonah: Crying Out for Help
When You're Desperate

1. Why do you think Jonah waited until he was in the belly of the fish to finally pray?

2. How do fear, failure, or feelings of inadequacy affect your prayer life?

3. What does Jonah's prayer teach us about God's mercy?

4. Can you think of a time when desperation made your prayers more real or raw?

5. How might Jonah's story encourage us when we feel like running from what God has asked of us?

Day 3 – Jesus: A Blueprint for Prayer
When You're Unsure

1. Why do you think Jesus warned against long, showy prayers?

2. Which part of the Lord's Prayer feels most personal to your life right now? Why?

3. How can the Lord's Prayer guide us when we feel stuck or unsure of what to say?

4. What does it look like to "surrender your plans" in daily life?

5. How could praying this way regularly shape your relationship with God?

6. Share a personal rewrite of the Lord's Prayer in your own words.

Day 4 – Everyday Prayer: Talking With God in Ordinary Moments

1. What does it mean to "pray continually" in your daily rhythm?

2. How have you experienced God in ordinary places—at home, at work, or on the go?

3. Why do you think God invites us into prayer in both big and small moments?

4. What is one everyday activity you could turn into prayer this week?

5. How might prayer change the way you approach ordinary responsibilities or challenges?

6. Share a story about a time when prayer surprised you in an unexpected place.

Day 5 – Prayer Is a Relationship: Drawing Near When You Need Peace

1. How does it change your perspective to see prayer as a relationship rather than a ritual?

2. What holds you back from praying freely and openly with God?

3. When have you experienced God's peace through prayer?

4. How does Philippians 4:6–7 encourage you in times of worry or anxiety?

5. What new prayer practice could you try this week to deepen your relationship with God?

6. How might consistent prayer shape your trust in God over time?

7. In your own words, what does it mean that "everyone needs a little Jesus"?

39

Philippians 4:6

"Do not be anxious about anything, but in every situation, by prayer and petition, with thanksgiving, present your requests to God."

Appendix D: Reader Bonus

Reader Bonus: A Gift for You

Want to keep growing in your prayer life?
Here's a simple resource just for you:

5 Ways to Pray: A Simple Guide

This easy-to-follow guide will show you five practical ways you can bring prayer into your everyday life, whether you're at home, at work, or on the go.

👉 To claim your free copy,

Go to <u>SallyLarkinGreen.com</u> and register today.

Sally Larkin Green

Meet the Author

Sally Larkin Green is an author, writing coach, and spiritual director who has spent over 30 years teaching and serving in her seaside hometown of Stratford, Connecticut. She preaches regularly at Lordship Community Church, a little white church with a big story. It was moved all the way from Vermont in 1950 and replanted by the shoreline as a testimony that faith is never meant to sit still.

That story of movement is at the heart of Sally's current ministry and writing. Just as the church was placed on wheels and brought into a new place, she believes faith is always calling us to take steps forward, draw closer to Jesus, and live with courage.

Sally is the author of multiple children's books, devotionals, and collaborative book projects that help everyday people share their stories. She is also a certified lay speaker who loves weaving scripture, humor, and personal experiences into her messages of encouragement and hope.

She lives with her husband Billy, her family nearby, and her 3 cats. She loves coffee, chocolate, and helping people discover that—truly—***everyone needs a little Jesus.***

Contact: <u>Sally@actiontakerspublishing.com</u>
Connect with Sally at: <u>FindSally.com</u>

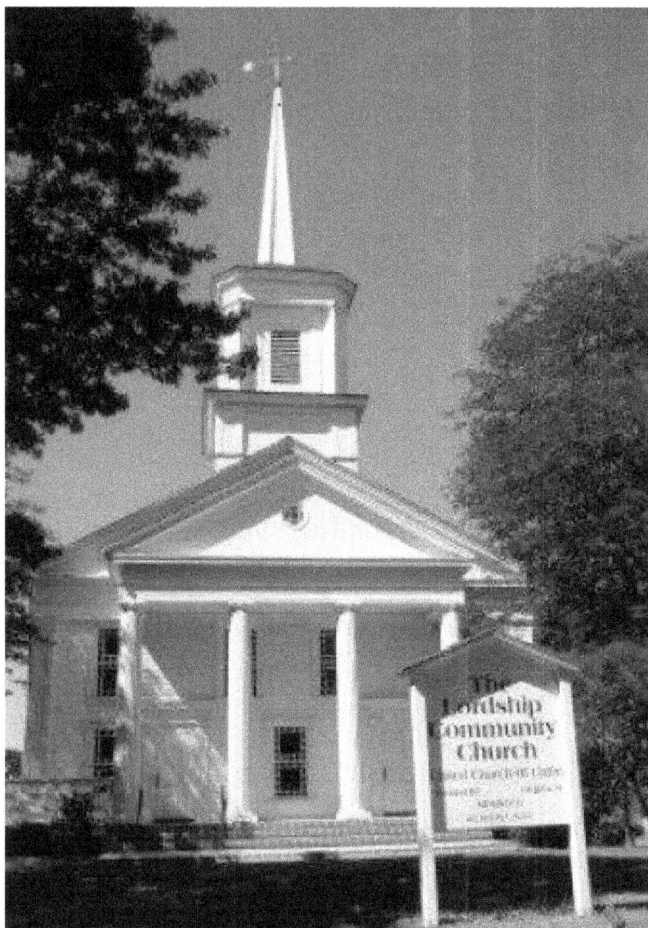

About Lordship Community Church

Lordship Community Church has a story of movement. Founded in 1922 as a small Sunday School, it grew until a church building was needed. In 1950, the little white church was moved from Vermont to Stratford, earning the nickname *"the church that moved away."* For generations, it has stood as a reminder that faith is never meant to sit still.

All are welcome to join us.

Worship Service: **Every Sunday at 10:00 AM**

Visit **TheLordshipChurch.org** to learn more about our services, outreach programs, and community events.

My Notes, Prayers and Reflections